Hovering In Harm's Way
A Marine Corps Pilot's
Journey to Vietnam and Back

By
Don Chretien

Copyright © 2017 Don Chretien
All rights reserved.

All rights reserved. No part of this publication may be reproduced, distributed, or transmitted in any form or by any means, including photocopying, recording, or other electronic or mechanical methods, without the prior written permission of the publisher, except in the case of brief quotations embodied in critical reviews and certain other noncommercial uses permitted by copyright law.

First Edition

ISBN-13:
978-1546878575

ISBN-10:
1546878572

14 13 12 11 10 / 10 9 8 7 6 5 4 3 2 1

DEDICATION

To all the Marine helicopter crews, especially the CH-46s, who continually responded to the needs of the U.S. Marine ground forces with supplies and evacuations to safety, while knowingly being exposed to enemy fire. Especially Marty Benson, a fellow CH-46 pilot from Wayzata, Minnesota, with whom I went through flight training. He gave his last full measure, as a co-pilot over the skies of Vietnam on February 6, 1970 during a troop insert.

To my wife, Ardis, daughters, Nicole, Shannon and my mother, for showing continual support and interest in my varied undertakings. For also bringing love to my life and making me proud of who you are, what you do, and how you do it.

To my grandchildren, Savannah, Hunter & Alex, for giving me a legacy for the future and another reason to write my Marine Corps memoirs.

CONTENTS

Prologue

Chapter 1   The Road to Pensacola

Chapter 2   Wings of Gold

Chapter 3   Helicopter Training

Chapter 4   Vietnam Tour of Duty

Chapter 5   The Road Home

Epilogue

Acknowledgements

Thanks to all the flight instructors and pilots who shared their skills with me and guided my development into a well-qualified Marine helicopter pilot.

Thanks to my squadron mates, especially Hank Lamb, Rick Grimstead and Rich Bell, who have continued to be my friends and helped me remember some facts and specifics during our shared Vietnam tour.

Thanks to Jack Feldt, a comrade, especially during our training and preparation while becoming helicopter pilots. You were great company and a comforting presence on the road to Vietnam. We always had a great time, especially on our "out of country" leaves to Hong Kong and Sidney, Australia. We helped each other keep things in perspective, and shared many laughs while staying reasonably out of trouble.

To Charlie Bassett, crew chief extraordinaire, who risked his life to come to my aid. If not for his action, I may not have experienced all of life's wonders, my deepest gratitude Charlie.

Last but not least, to David Arenstam, a local published author, without him I could not have achieved getting this manuscript into a printable format. His expert guidance and encouragement helped me get my story published. Many thanks, David.

Foreword

My lifelong dream was to become a pilot. As a young boy, I remember watching planes flying overhead and thinking I wanted to do that. Strange as it may seem now, I had never actually flown in an aircraft, and yet I felt it was my calling. My plan to accomplish this goal was to get a college degree, and armed with a diploma, I would qualify for military flight school.

My dreams became a reality when I signed a five-year commitment for military service and joined the United States Marine Corps. I served from 1967-1972 as a helicopter pilot, but for the first two years of my commitment I trained and transitioned from a civilian fresh out of the University of Maine to a fully qualified military aviator.

Why am I telling my story now, 47 years after my tour in Vietnam? For years, I looked for books and stories about the Marine CH-46 helicopter pilots and crew's perspectives about the Vietnam War. I looked for memoirs, biographies, and tales about the bases and duty stations where I flew, about the men who trained with me, and about Marine aviation. I didn't find a lot and now, before it was too late, I wanted to tell my story, our story.

Now that it is finished, I can say the process has been cathartic and long overdue. Like many of the men and women who served during that time, I had not openly shared these stories, but it's time.

CHAPTER 1

THE ROAD TO PENSACOLA

Late winter in Maine can be a tough time of the year. There's always the chance of snow, rain, or the increasing likelihood that the streets and walkways will be covered in dirt and mud. For me, my worries and thoughts had nothing to do with the weather. I was concerned about the war and my draft status. In 1967, the last semester of my senior year at the University of Maine, Orono, I was only taking three classes and working to help with my tuition and living expenses. With this reduced class load, the university and the government did not consider me a full-time student, and that meant I was available for the draft. There seemed to be little doubt that I'd spend some time in a uniform, but I wanted to avoid being drafted and enter the military service on my own terms, hopefully that meant pilot training.

Initially I approached an Air Force recruiter to find out about the qualifications needed to become a pilot. After some discussion, I was told they only recruited engineers for pilots. However, I could possibly qualify to become a missile silo officer. That did not sound like something I wanted to do, so I approached one of the Navy recruiters. They gave me a battery of tests to evaluate my mechanical and academic abilities. I achieved the necessary scores to join the service and I qualified for a slot as an aviation candidate. But the Navy would not sign me until I graduated with a degree. Knowing I would probably get drafted before that happened, I decided to make a trip to see the Marine Corps recruiter to find out what he could do for me.

Finally I had some luck. Because the Marine Corps trained pilots through the Navy flight program, and I had already passed all of the necessary tests, I was qualified to potentially become a Marine pilot. All I had to do was sign an advanced acceptance into the Marine Corps for a five-year service commitment - standard contract for pilot training. My name and service number would no longer be available for the draft and I'd belong to the Marine Corps. After graduation from the University of Maine I would be sent to Quantico, Virginia for OCS (Officer's Candidate School). If successful in earning my lieutenant bars, I was guaranteed a spot in the Naval Aviation Flight Training Program in Pensacola, Florida. My decision seemed easy, and after a few simple signatures, I began my Marine Corps service.

For the first time since kindergarten, I wasn't going to school in the fall. This 23-year-old young man from Biddeford was heading to Marine OCS in Quantico, Virginia. As the Red Sox made their improbable run toward the world series, I was packing, saying goodbye to family and friends, and wondering what boot camp and flight training would be like.

I found OCS basic training to be quite challenging, interesting and amusing at times. It was physically and mentally difficult, yet stimulating. The drill sergeants used the continual threat of failure or DOR (Dismissed On Request), to motivate individuals who started to fall behind. It was simple, if we washed out of OCS, we would be sent to Parris Island to complete boot camp and become a Marine enlisted man. But I had an edge. My last roommate in college was a former Staff Sergeant in the Corps, and he trained me well for the upcoming demands of boot camp. I was in the best physical condition of my life.

The physical and mental pressure in basic training did prove to be troublesome for some but I found the experience challenging and fascinating. I kept thinking about the road ahead and my plans to fly. It seems funny now, but I was frequently criticized by my platoon commander and drill sergeant for looking like I was having too good a time.

"Chretien, take that shit-eating grin off your face or I'll take it off," the drill sergeant would bark in my direction.

I am in the fourth row, far right side

At one point, on a forced march, we were going up a dirt slope under slippery, snowy, winter conditions. The weather reminded me of home and when most of my platoon slipped and started to fall behind, I moved faster and faster until I began to pass the leader, our platoon commander, a 1st Lieutenant and former enlisted man. He wasn't having any of that.

He grabbed me by the collar, pulled me back and advised me to never try passing him again. That incident seems funny now but I took that advice to heart and avoided any repercussions. Eventually, I earned the honor of representing my platoon for the obstacle course race, and I won that event with the best time in the Company. After three months of rigorous training I earned my 2nd

Lieutenant bars. Our drill sergeant was given the honor of pinning those bars on us and he was the first person to salute us as officers. After so many weeks in basic training, it was a thrill to be addressed as "Sir" by our tough as nails instructor.

There was pressure placed on every hopeful flight training candidate during the last couple of weeks of boot camp. The highest honor for the Marines was supposedly to serve as a platoon commander with a ground combat unit. About the time I graduated from OCS there was a desperate need for 2nd lieutenants. The high casualty rate of these individuals in Vietnam was well known. I had no illusions of grandeur regarding the honor of remaining after boot camp to attend "The Basic School." This was further combat leadership training for newly appointed officers to lead ground troops.

Those who finished this training were assigned to a unit in Vietnam within six months, and it just so happened that 1968 was one of the most active periods of the war. The Tet Offensive and the siege of Khe Sanh started at the end of January and lasted for months. I do not know the casualty rate among my fellow boot camp platoon mates who became infantry officers, but, the Marine rifle platoon officers casualty and wounded rate during the Vietnam War was very high, some sources indicate it approached 85 percent.

CHAPTER 2

Wings of Gold

I graduated from OCS in February 1968, and I was thrilled to be off to sunny Pensacola and Navy flight training. When I arrived there was a three month waiting period before the start of flight school. I was given a TAD (Temporary Additional Duty) assignment as one of the defensive driving instructors for the airbase. My partner in this assignment was another Marine Lieutenant from Kentucky. I must say we had a good time conducting those classes for military personnel who had been cited for a motor vehicle violation on base. Since my partner had a deep southern accent, and I had a New England accent, we played off each other, and took turns presenting material. We tried to lessen the pain of having to take these classes, and often, we had the attendees laughing along with our antics.

As temporary instructors, we only had classes for a few hours each week so we had plenty of spare time on our hands. I enjoyed going to the beach and snorkeling off Santa Rosa Island, as well as, starting to play some golf on the base course, and partying quite a bit. It was my first exposure to Florida and "southern belles." The saying regarding southern hospitality was evident with every smile, especially for an "officer and gentleman by act of Congress" (that moniker is part of our officer certificates).

Once I started flight training, things got very serious and a great deal of focus and attention were required. The time for parties and the girls was over. I was competing with many other guys who dreamed of flying jets, and in order to qualify for jets you had to score well in ground school classes, and then perform well in the air. We started with ground school classes that were focused on aeronautics. The material in the classes taught us every detail of why aircraft manage to fly through the sky. We were taught the physics of airflow over the wings and how pitch, roll, and yaw are used for desired flight control. Intermingled with the details of flight were the physical training programs. These essential programs included parachute training, cockpit evacuation, and water survival training.

Parachute training was performed from a tower in one of the base's back bays and the base of the tower was on the Gulf of Mexico. Each trainee was in a parachute harness in a tower attached to a long cable leading to the water at a 30 degree angle. Since we were to become Naval Aviators, water landings with parachute needed to be mastered. The key to a successful ditching at sea was how to get free from the chute after landing without getting entangled. Just prior to hitting the water, a pilot needed to detach from the parachute harness and once in the water, the pilot needed to swim away from it to avoid the hundreds of lines and the canvas itself.

Another training segment was the cockpit evacuation drill. This took place in an indoor pool using the "Dilbert Dunker". It was a mock cockpit that was on a set of rails which led into the pool. You were buckled into the cockpit with lap and shoulder straps as in any aircraft.

Once signaled ready, the cockpit slid down the railing crashing into the water. As it immersed deep into the pool the cockpit flipped forward and inverted. The trainee had to unbuckle the harness and swim downward to clear the cockpit before trying to reach the surface, while holding his breath. There were some trainees who had to be rescued from this drill when they either panicked or could not extricate themselves in a timely fashion. Divers stood by to help anyone needing assistance. Personally, I loved these drills and if allowed, I would have done them over and over again.

We also had to prove our ability to survive in the water. This was done through long swims around the pool, having to float for long periods of time without life vests or contact with the pool's edge. Poor swimmers were especially challenged by these drills and potentially could wash out of flight school, if unable to eventually learn to swim long enough to pass the practical exam.

Finally, once pilot candidates successfully completed ground school, we started training in actual aircraft. As a group we were anxious to experience real flight and we started at NAS (Naval Air Station) Saufley Field in Pensacola, Florida. Our first aircraft was the T-34, Mentor. It was a small, propeller driven, two-seater (front and rear). Manufactured by Beechcraft Bonanza, it was powered by a Lycoming 0-470-13 piston engine, and its top speed was around 200 mph. It was a forgiving plane with a manually operated canopy that slid forward to enclose the cockpit, but could be flown either open or closed. The flight instructor sat in the rear seat, giving guidance and monitoring our every move. I had "white knuckle syndrome" for some time during initial training. That's when one is so focused and tense trying to do well, that I had a death grip on the flight stick, indicated by white knuckles. That resulted in less than smooth handling of the aircraft. I recall having difficulty with landing by "porpoising" (bouncing up and down) as we approached the runway and floated in ground-effect (the layer or cushion of air below the wings and above the runway). Ground effect caused the plane to bounce back into the air if the airspeed and approach angle were not appropriate. One could not force this aircraft to the ground until the airspeed was slow enough for it to settle to the runway. It was a real challenge to remember all the details and checklists that needed to be addressed in that first segment of training. During one memorable check flight (a test to go to next stage), I forgot to close the canopy once reaching cruise altitude. The instructor asked me to point out a particular landmark. As I extended my arm out of the cockpit and the wind stream pulled it violently back against the canopy, it dawned on me what I had forgotten. I had a few remedial lessons in order to finally solo (fly without an instructor), but I did eventually manage to get there.

Jack and I (atop the wing) T-34 Mentor

Since I was competing with many guys who already had their private pilot's licenses, or many hours in the air, my flight scores were not competitive. When we finished with the T-34 training portion, the selection process for two separate pipelines was announced. At the time, the Vietnam War demands were heavily skewed for helicopter positions. Therefore, 85% of our class was given the helicopter pipeline. Only those scoring very high in flight training were selected for the jet pipeline. Although initially disappointed, I was very pleased to have made it through such demanding training without the benefit of prior flight experience.

We, who were given the helicopter pipeline, then began further training in the North American Aviation's T-28 Trojan aircraft. This was a much larger, much more powerful, single engine, fixed wing, propeller aircraft. It was a two-seater (front & rear) powered by a Wright R-1820-86 Cyclone radial engine, producing 1,425 horsepower with a max speed of 343 mph. It had a ceiling altitude of 39,000 feet but since we did not have oxygen on board, we were limited to 10,000 feet. The T-28 was a difficult aircraft to handle at first, but after a few hours in the cockpit, it became a real pleasure to fly, because it had great flight performance characteristics. It was also used during the war for close air support, mainly by the South Vietnamese. We went through several flight training stages; aircraft familiarity, solo, instruments, formation flying, acrobatics, and finally aircraft carrier qualification.

Boarding the T-28 Trojan for a training flight

Getting accustomed to this powerful plane was eye opening. Once cleared to take off by the control tower, going to full throttle while holding the brakes to maintain position to check the engine's readiness for flight, was an amazing experience. You could feel the aircraft straining under the engine's power. Once releasing the brakes, it almost seemed to jump forward as it roared down the runway. I remember the aircraft shaking and shuttering as it rolled down the tarmac as I tried to maintain center line heading with the foot pedals. When takeoff airspeed was attained, it jumped off the runway and quickly climbed to the desired altitude.

At first things happened faster than I could keep up with, considering the number of things that needed to be done soon after liftoff. The gear had to be retracted, as well as, maintaining a reasonable climbing rate via power and pitch angle (nose up position). Then adjusting the trim wheel to more easily handle the flight control surfaces (foot pedals for yaw, stick for pitch and roll, throttle for smooth transition to assigned altitude and cruising speed). All that while also talking to the control tower and the instructor. After a few flights those things became automatic. We were then expected to accurately control specific altitude and compass direction during turns, airspeed and flight level changes. We also practiced recovering from stalls (loss of lift from slow airspeed and/or excess turn rate, called approach turn stall). Landings were also expected to get "greased" (very smooth touchdown) on the runway centerline.

Once mastering basic maneuvers, we were challenged to deal with emergency procedures. The flight instructor would pull circuit breakers and judge our reaction to varying emergency situations. All these were covered in pre-flight discussions and instructor demonstrations before being surprised by them during flight. However, one never knew when a circuit breaker was going to be pulled or what indication needed to be detected to recognize the emergency situation. That was difficult while still having to continue monitoring all the other flight gauges and controls.

Once satisfactorily dealing with these situations, I was authorized to solo. It was a great feeling to be given the opportunity to fly this high performing aircraft by myself, and I loved it. To be in and around the clouds diving, climbing and turning at will was a wondrous feeling. I had dreamed about it as a young boy, and I cherished every moment of that freedom.

During a solo flight, I decided to see if I could reach 300 knots in a dive, which I did. It was invigorating and scary at the same time. This was an old aircraft, albeit very well maintained, it still had been in training service for many years and probably abused by many young pilots. We heard stories of some very high "g" (positive or negative gravity) maneuvers completed by solo pilots, which caused the aircraft's skin to ripple. This was not something the instructors encouraged or approved.

The next segment of training was instrument flying under "the bag." A canvas covering was draped over the trainee's canopy. There was no reference to the outside and you had to guide the aircraft to a destination strictly through the use of instruments. The flight instructor would take the plane off, get to a safe altitude, and the trainee had to follow the instruments to a destination. I vividly remember one particular flight when I was directed to find the ILS (Instrument Landing System) outer marker. I was flying perpendicular to the marker location and had to watch for the instrument indicator to move, which would signal the outer marker's location. At cruising speed, this happens very quickly especially since you're monitoring a number of other flight gauges, at the same time trying to hold airspeed, altitude and direction. I missed the indicator three times in a row, as we went back and forth. At that point, the flight instructor noted that I was getting low on fuel and asked what I would do next. I told him that I would bail out. He was not pleased with that response and I had another remedial session.

During this segment we were also exposed to the effects of vertigo in flight. The instructor had me close my eyes and turn my head to one side. He then placed the aircraft in a sharp turn. When asked to open my eyes and take control of the aircraft, I was totally disoriented. He asked me to return the aircraft to level flight. When I attempted to do it, my body and mind deceived me into feeling the instruments were wrong. I began to make adjustments that were incorrect. The instruments indicated I was losing airspeed and climbing while my body told me I was still in a turn. It was weird and a lesson well learned. Believe your instruments and not your senses when flying without view of the horizon, as in clouds or under "the bag".

Formation flying was a thrill to practice. Detail explanations before, during and after flight, were essential. Flying in close formation with another aircraft is very precise and requires constant subtle adjustments in power and attitude (pitch & roll). The rendezvous occurs by flying in a circular pattern inside the turn of the lead aircraft. Closure rate is difficult to judge and can be dangerous. If one closes too quickly, a collision could occur since you're both at the same altitude. Once you have joined up on the lead aircraft's lower back side, there are several reference points on his aircraft that you use to keep the proper position on his wing. A high degree of concentration on the lead aircraft and therefore intuitive control changes go into maintaining proper position. One of the rewards for successfully completing this segment was flying in formation over the runway and breaking (90 degree turn) one at a time for landing. I felt like I was a Blue Angel for a moment. What a thrill.

Acrobatics, although difficult, was a lot of fun. By this time we had quite a few hours logged in the T-28 and we're very proficient at controlling the aircraft in regular flight. Now the further challenge was learning how to control it during more extreme maneuvers. We did vertical stalls, wing overs, barrel rolls, loops and Immelmanns (half loop, half roll), all adding to our mastery of the aircraft. Many of these maneuvers were used during dog fights in WWII, but for our purposes they were to increase our confidence and skills at controlling and recovering the aircraft while in a variety of attitudes.

The final T-28 training segment was carrier qualification. This was, by far, the most exciting and challenging part of the program for me. We practiced on a regular runway which was marked with the outline of a carrier flight deck. We had to land within the confines of lines drawn on the landing area representing arresting cables. There are a series of 4 large cables stretched across the flight deck. The aircraft's tail hook is to grab onto one of them once you've landed on the deck. It's a lot harder landing than normal because of the short landing area on the carrier deck and the need to maintain flying airspeed just before cutting power. After demonstrating the ability to land within the second and third cables with reasonable regularity, we were deemed ready for the real thing.

Arrested landing with the first or fourth cables were not favored. A slight miscalculation for the first cable could have you hit the fantail (rear of the ship) and ruin your day. The fourth cable was discouraged because of the possibility that the hook could bounce over the cable. That could have you being fished out of the ocean. To avoid this scenario, you had to cut the power to idle for landing, and once you made contact with the deck, you had to immediately go to full power in case of a cable skip. This would hopefully allow you to return to flying airspeed before running out of flight deck.

Flying out to the carrier, I saw a tiny, rolling and pitching deck in the middle of the Gulf of Mexico. I knew I was supposed to land on that small gray piece of steel. That got my attention, but I felt well prepared. We actually went out three times before we actually tried a landing because of inclement weather (low ceiling and excess deck pitch and roll).

My first carrier landing in a T-28

I eventually qualified with three successful tail hook arrested landings and take offs on the carrier USS Lexington (a WWII vintage carrier). Even after being warned in training, I was amazed at the quick stop that occurs when going from flight speed to arrested landing. My mind could not process how quickly that happened. One moment you're flying and the next you're sitting on the deck with your engine at full throttle. At the same time, a deck hand is waving at you to pull back on the power so that they can release the cable. Then, just as quickly, the deck hand is waving at you to take off, since another aircraft is in the pattern getting ready to land right behind you. We did not use a catapult to take off, since we could get to flight speed on the flight deck. I would have loved to be catapulted, but only the jet pilots got to experience that thrill.

Once we successfully completed carrier qualifications, we were awarded our Gold Naval Flight Wings. I was thrilled. It took a total of two years of hard work to get those wings, and get totally qualified in my designated aircraft. I was damn proud of it.

A proud day. Mother pinning on my Naval Wings At NAS Pensacola, Florida

CHAPTER 3

Helicopter Training

Helicopter pilots went on to train at NAS Whiting Field in Milton, Florida. First we trained in the Bell Jet Ranger (TH-57), then the Bell UH-1 (Huey) helicopter. My first hover attempt in the Jet Ranger was pretty scary. I was all over the sky. Trying to control the three axes of roll, pitch and yaw, while hovering, is quite a feat. But, after a few hours of practice, I started to get the knack of it.

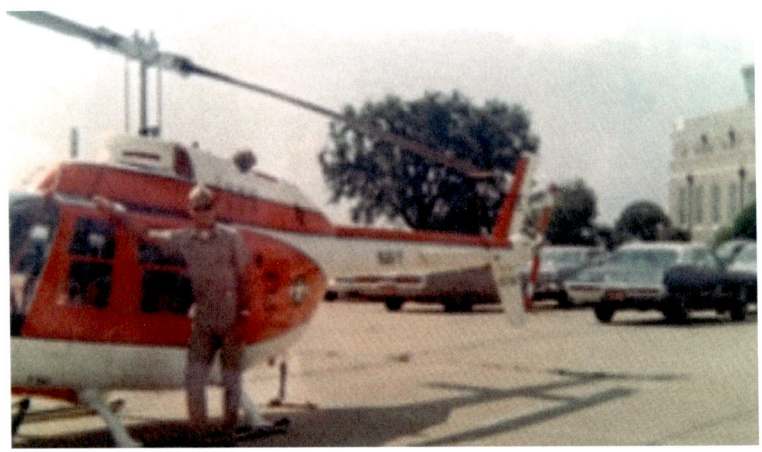

The TH-57 Bell Jet Ranger

An essential technique taught to helicopter pilots is auto-rotation. This is a method unique to helicopter flight that allows us to land reasonably safely without engine power. It is practiced quite a bit to ensure a pilot is confident and capable enough to complete the maneuver without endangering the crew and passengers in an emergency and still land safely. Pilots refer to it as "a controlled crash." During practice, it involves lowering the collective (power control) to idle and gliding down from altitude controlling the direction of the aircraft with only the two flight controls (stick for pitch and roll, foot rudder pedals for yaw). A landing spot is chosen and without the use of engine power one has to direct the helo toward the ground. Within a recommended distance from touchdown (varies with size and weight of the helicopter), the pilot pulls back on the flight stick to raise the nose of the aircraft, simultaneously pulling up on the collective to use the still spinning rotor blades to increase lift capability. The rotors continue to turn without power because of the air flow through the rotor blades as you descend creates a pinwheel effect. If done correctly, it slows the copter's descent rate and increases lift enough to partially cushion the landing, minimizing impact. In training the engine is never turned off and power is used at the end of the maneuver to avoid frequent excessive impact to the training helicopters.

The Bell UH-1 (Huey)

Once we had soloed in the Jet Ranger, we went on to the "Huey". More practice with hovering, landing, taxiing and auto-rotation. But now we were flying an actual combat helicopter being heavily used in Vietnam. Things were getting closer to reality and what our future purpose would potentially become beyond training.

After a few weeks of basic helicopter training, we were assigned a specific aircraft. I was transferred to MCAS (Marine Corps Air Station) New River in Jacksonville, NC for the rest of my training in the CH-46, my designated aircraft. This was a much larger helicopter powered by twin jet engines. It was nicknamed, "Phrog," because it was all green and looked like a frog while sitting in place. It is a tandem rotor, cigar-shaped helicopter that performed a multitude of duties.

The 46 could transport up to 24 troops, depending on the equipment being carried and the temperature and the altitude of the landing zone. All those parameters had to be calculated in advance, to ensure a safe flight. Troops could parachute out the rear ramp or rappel down wires hanging to the ground. This is done when there is insufficient landing space or need for a quick troop insert. Once we had become familiar with this chopper and were able to control it from takeoff to landing and hovering, we then began to

A CH-46 in a revetment for protecting aircraft in Vietnam

learn more operational techniques vital to its role.
It was critical to learn combat type maneuvers from flight instructors who had recently returned from a tour of duty in Vietnam. An example of a combat technique is controlling

the descent over a Landing Zone (LZ) with minimum exposure to ground areas beyond that zone. This method is used when there is no safe area (North, South, East or West) to approach from to get to the LZ because of enemy activity or terrain. It involves placing the helicopter in an unbalanced state of flight. Power to the engines is reduced to idle, the nose is pitched down and the aircraft is placed in a banked turn, while pushing the rudder (yaw foot pedal) in the opposite direction of the turn. That places the chopper in a side slip mode (moving through the air sideways instead of forward), and the descent is limited to the area directly over the LZ. One can feel the air flow through the side windows of the airframe. That process results in an extremely high rate of descent, and limiting exposure to enemy fire. As you approach the LZ, power is brought back and balanced flight is restored for landing. It is a very uncomfortable state of flight but works very well.

Marines rappelling from a hovering CH-46

Another critical training was interpreting map coordinates for navigation purposes, and taking cross country trips to experience air traffic control. Jack (good friend and my roommate during this period of training) and I took trips to Columbus Ohio and also to Pease Air Force Base in Portsmouth, NH, with an instructor, alternating turns as copilot. On the latter trip, we spent the weekend in Maine, visiting my folks, and going to our cottage on the lake. It was a very relaxing weekend, and we all had a great time enjoying a summer weekend in my home state. During the Maine trip, we made an instrument approach landing to NAS (Naval Air Station) South Weymouth, MA for refueling and then to Logan airport in Boston to drop off a passenger. It was interesting dealing with the control tower at Logan since they are more accustomed to airline traffic and not military helicopters. As we were on final approach, they asked us to increase our airspeed because of the reduced separation with an incoming passenger jet following us for landing. The instructor informed them that we were at maximum cruise speed (120 knots) and could not go any faster. As a result, they had us change our approach to a taxiway, since we could come to a hover and did not need the long roll out after landing that passenger planes require.

I have fond and funny memories of that trip to Maine. My parents picked us up at Pease AFB in Portsmouth, New Hampshire. They surprised us by stopping and treating us to a lobster dinner at Valley's Steak House in

Kittery, Maine. We had all brought civilian clothes to change into, but we were still wearing our flight suits. We had left thinking we'd change when we got to my home. During the dinner, some lobster juice was spilled onto our flight suits, and with everything going on, we did not think of getting them cleaned. We just threw them in the trunk of the car for the weekend. It was summer, and the heat had quite an effect on those suits. When we got back to Pease, and had to change back into them, the odor was incredible. All heads were turned as we walked into flight operations to file our flight plan back to Jacksonville, NC.

By late fall of 1969, I had completed all the essential training in the CH-46, and was ready for my first active, non-training, duty assignment. We had been assured at each segment of our training, that most likely the Vietnam War would be over by the time we were ready for an overseas tour. Therefore, our orders for West Pac (Western Pacific) seemed quite foreboding when they were received. The next three years of my military commitment were now ahead of me, and I was just a 25-year-old young man from Maine.

I went home on leave before my overseas departure. I left home shortly after Thanksgiving and before Christmas. My family celebrated both holidays with me before I left. It was comforting to know in advance that I would be returning home for Christmas with family after my 12-month overseas tour ended.

My last stop before departing the states was in Southern California. My buddy Jack's sister lived in Huntington Beach and we were invited to a "going away" party for us at their home. She was a teacher at a local elementary school, and arranged for a fellow teacher, Ardis, to attend. I had a great time talking at the party with Ardis, and really enjoyed her company. I made sure, before I left, that I had her address so that I could write to her while overseas. I felt she was a very special person, and wanted to get to know more about this lovely young lady.

The next day, Jack and I went to Disneyland, and actually rode the Magic Kingdom ride "Small World" together. What a hoot, two Marines sitting on that ride with a lot of other much younger people. Early the next morning we were scheduled to depart for an unspecified overseas destination.

CHAPTER 4

Vietnam – Tour of Duty

My first thought of an ominous sign, was when leaving the U.S. for a potential war zone assignment, in the early morning of December 7, 1969. My educational background in history, made me fully aware of, "a date that will live in infamy," quoted by FDR after the bombing of Pearl Harbor, in the early morning of December 7, 1941. When we arrived in Okinawa, which was the distribution point for Far East assignments, we were given our orders and ultimate destination. Both Jack and I were headed to Vietnam for the next 12 months.

I deeply regret not having kept a personal daily log of my activities during my 12 months in Vietnam. It was a time in my life when I had achieved my fondest dream, I had become a Marine officer and pilot. It was also a time when I had to face my greatest challenge, performing while being in harm's way. I have tried to recall some of the more memorable moments, but I know that time has filtered out many specific experiences while "in country" (term for being in Vietnam).

We were transported to Da Nang, in the northernmost sector of South Vietnam, called I Corps. Jack and I traveled together during this period, which was very comforting. We were both assigned to 1st Marine Air Wing, Marine Air Group-16, HMM-364 (Helicopter Marine Medium).

Our base was at Marble Mountain Air facility, on the beach of the South China Sea, just south of Da Nang. It was almost exclusively a helicopter facility. A bleak appearing environment, compared to what we had been accustomed. Our introductory evening included a middle of the night B-40 enemy rocket attack on the base. The ground shook and it felt like they were falling just outside my hut, but in fact, they had all fallen short of the base. I was shaken and thought, what am I doing here, and is this going to be a regular part of my 12 month stay here in country? Actually, that was the last rocket attack I remember, other than a few mortar attacks during the rest of my tour.

Marble Mountain Air Facility, Vietnam

"swifty" our squadron mascot

Each squadron had its own special insignia and call sign to represent its pilots and crews. My squadron, HMM-364, was known as the "Purple Foxes." We had a picture of a purple fox with our motto "give a shit" (indicating we cared), painted on both sides of the rear rotor pylon. Our call sign on the radio was "Yankee Kilo", followed by whichever aircraft number you were flying on a mission. There was great comradery in our squadron and we had minimal losses for the time I was in Vietnam (Dec. 1969-Dec. 1970). During my tour, we did lose a couple of aircraft. One aircraft and its entire crew were lost when it struck a mountain peak at cruising speed during bad weather. Another pilot was killed by enemy fire during an emergency extract from a "hot LZ" (Landing Zone with enemy fire). Both were tragic losses, but comparatively, it wasn't too bad a ratio for a 46-squadron, considering our exposure and the number of missions flown on a daily basis.

Our mission "in country" was quite varied. We did resupplies, troop inserts, emergency extracts (getting troops out of heavy firefights), day and night medivacs (transporting wounded troops to medical aid stations), and reconnaissance missions to oversee potential enemy areas or activity. We also flew a few administrative flights; I took

Cardinal Cook to a Bob Hope USO show, flew troops to their assigned posts and back to return home or for R&R, delivered hot turkey dinners and beer to troops in the field on Thanksgiving & Christmas, brought ice cream to troops in the bush during the hot summer, and delivered C-rations to hungry native children.

On average, we flew 4-8 hours a day and experienced a sea of routine flights, with hours of inactivity while on hold, amid flashes of hair raising missions. We also performed triple canopy extracts, which included hovering over thick trees and foliage, where landing was impossible. For quick troop extracts, sometimes a ladder (steel cables with metal rungs) was used. For even narrower openings in trees, we used "SPIE rigs" (Special Patrol Insert/Extract), a large single steel cable with four pairs of rings attached toward the bottom, eight feet or so apart,

for troops to quickly hook onto their harnesses. Those cables hung 100 feet or so from the chopper's "hell hole" (a trap door at the lower center of the aircraft), and where the crew chief guided us over the extract location.

Even after more than four decades, I remember looking at a Stars & Stripes (military newspaper in country) cartoon. It depicted a pilot talking to his copilot from a hovering helicopter over a hot LZ. It pictured the copter with multiple holes penetrating it from enemy fire. The pilot commenting, "I wish I was down there, wishing I was up here." That graphically described the situation during our tour. We were envied for our daily living accommodations. We lived in air conditioned housing on the South China Sea beach. That area was considered in-country R&R (Rest and Re-cooperation) for the ground troops. But, the times when we were hovering over a hot LZ, while taking enemy fire, one felt like a sitting duck, unable to run or hide. We were not envied then.

Thank God for the cover frequently provided by Marine Cobras (attack helicopters with awesome fire power), and Huey gunships. They definitely helped keep enemy heads down during some of these missions. The Cobra's 2-barrel, 7.62mm Gatling gun alone could cover every square foot of a football field with a round in 30 seconds. Incredible!

AH-1 Cobra – Two-man helicopter (gunner in front and pilot in rear) Armament – two 7.62mm Gatling guns and 4 rocket pods housing 44 rockets

We also had two 50-caliber machine guns, one on each side of the 46, manned by two gunners. You could see trees falling over from the impact of those large caliber bullets. The helicopter shook when they were being fired, but it was comforting to hear and feel the vibration of those guns, when we made approaches to hot landing zones. Both pilot and co-pilot had armor plated seats that gave some protection from directly below and partially from the side. However, one still felt quite exposed from the front where there was nothing but plexiglass and aluminum sheet metal, which offered negligible protection from even small arms fire.

Pilots were housed in hooches, which were metal framed Quonset huts, shaped like half of a tube. They were divided into four separate quarters, two men per room. We were situated right next to the South China Sea Beach. During our off hours, we worked our way around openings in defensive concertina wire to access the beach. We would lie in the sun, swim, and body surf the waves. They even had surf boards available, if we wished to use them. That was pretty good duty for a war zone.

My "hooch" – right front building left side door

Our food for the first half of my tour was supplied by the Navy. They fed us well, and the chow was pretty good, most of the time. However, during the second half of my tour, the Army took over our food supplies. Both the quality and taste went substantially downhill.

In the evening, when we weren't assigned to night duties, we could go to the Officers' Club for drinks and at times live entertainment, usually on weekends. The bands, with singers and dancers, were mostly Vietnamese. Although they tried hard to mimic current popular American music and songs, it was never quite right with their Asian accents. A favorite song at the time and especially in country was, "we gotta get out of this place," by Eric Burdon and the Animals. It was requested and heard very often and represented the sentiments of most military personnel in Vietnam. Protesters back home were not the only ones who did not want us to be there. After a while we yearned to see "round eye" (Caucasian) entertainers. I can remember the guys going nuts when an Australian group came to our club and entertained. The female lead singer, by the end of the evening, was covered with insignia pins from all the squadrons, pinned all over the front of her dress. Everyone was delighted to see and hear a group sing without an Asian accent.

Our daily routine consisted of a wakeup call to both the pilot and copilot by the O.D. (Officer of the Day), which could come well before dawn, depending on the mission. We'd put on our flight suits and side arms (I carried a 45-caliber pistol), and get breakfast in the Officers' Mess Hall. Then, we were transported by open truck called "6-BYs" (because they were six wheel drive) to the Squadron Ready Room, where the mission assignments were noted on a white board.

Ready Room - Mission Assignment Board

We'd get briefed on our mission, the coordinates of where we were to fly, the radio contact frequency and call sign of the unit. In addition, we received reports on the status of troops or enemy activity. We'd put on our flak jackets, grab our flight helmets, and take the needed maps out to the flight line. We'd meet with the crew chief (enlisted man assigned to a specific helicopter and its maintenance), and get updated on the condition of his aircraft. We'd then perform an inspection of the chopper before entering the cockpit. As we ran through our checklist to start the aircraft, other personnel or equipment potentially assigned to the mission were loaded on board. This could include; a corpsman (enlisted Navy medical personnel), two gunners, troops and equipment.

The crew chief was always last to board, ensuring we had everyone aboard and everything looked good after engines start and rotors turning. We would then get clearance from the control tower, taxi out to the runway, roll out and lift off. As soon as we were airborne, we would call into DASC (Direct Air Support Center) in Da Nang, to report our departure for the mission and receive any updates. Once arriving "on station" (specified location), we would radio the ground operator, to acknowledge the landing area, and get confirmation that he could hear or see us overhead. If unclear or in heavy vegetation, we then would ask them to "pop a smoke" (ignite a smoke grenade).

We would always visually, and over the radio, confirm the color of that smoke. That process had become standard operating procedure, after a number of smoke grenades were released by the enemy to attract helicopters into an ambush. It was also important to get a visual check of the wind velocity and direction. It is best to land into the wind, if possible, to assist in maintaining as much lift as possible to land or hover. The exception was if there was enemy activity downwind and a recommendation to avoid a particular area on approach from the ground personnel was advised.

Some missions were considered more dangerous than others, depending on where we were headed, enemy (referred to as "Charlie") activity, or condition of the landing zone. We equally shared all missions. No one got a pass on more difficult ones because of a concern for safety, marital status, or having dependent children back home.

Night medivac was one of the more challenging missions. We'd spend the night in a medivac hut, on call for the entire night. It was so dark in Vietnam, because of the lack of any lights out in the bush, that on cloudy nights, you could not see your hand in front of your face. In the cockpit we had red lighting, which is better for maintaining night vision, and a must to see all the controls and gauges. Once we'd arrived at the coordinates given to us for the emergency (did not fly at night unless someone was in critical condition), we would ask for a flare or strobe light from the ground to pinpoint the landing area. When needed for safety, we'd turn on our search light once within 500 feet of the ground to get a visual reference for final landing. At night we used as little lighting as possible, since lights attracted enemy fire. I once had to land in elephant grass that was nearly 10 feet tall. It was very unsettling, not being able to see the ground under the grass. I landed on a large bolder which caused the chopper to pitch to one side. I had to quickly regain control into a hover, and move over a few feet to land safely.

Wounded troops were taken to secure area medical facilities in country or at sea, depending on the availability, distance and criticality. DASC would make that decision once we checked in with them after getting airborne and reporting the condition of wounded aboard.

Hospital Ship "Sanctuary" in Da Nang Harbor
HMM-364 Chopper dropping off wounded

Other challenging missions required "ramp landings". The 46 had a rear ramp, approximately 6 by 6 feet, for troop or cargo discharge. We flew with the ramp up until it was time to offload. When the LZ was in a narrow or severely slanted area, that was not wide enough to set the copter down completely, we would have to back in. Often, we'd hover with our rear ramp down, and the only contact with the ground was that ramp or just the rear wheels. The helicopter pilot's skill at hovering was absolutely essential on these occasions. You had to hold your position long enough for the troops to be able to get in or to the ground, without having them jump too far up or down, to avoid potential falls and injuries. Your visual reference during a hover was not the ground but the horizon. The crew chief had to guide you in until you contacted the ground. I once did this with a 3,000 foot drop in front of the nose of the aircraft. That's when your skills and nerves were tested. As you can imagine, a crew chief was an extremely vital person on the aircraft. We counted heavily on him for our safe landings. We could not see directly under or behind the aircraft from the cockpit so he was our eyes and guide into the LZ.

We all were very close to our crew chiefs since we entrusted our lives to them as they did with us. They were usually 19 or 20-year-old NCOs (Non-Commissioned Officers, mostly corporals and sergeants), and were an absolutely integral part of our team. The crew chiefs had a lot of responsibility. They maintained their own aircraft, enjoyed their role and were shown great respect by pilots. Many of the crew chiefs re-upped for additional tours because they did not relish the idea of returning to the "spit & polish", loss of freedom and strict discipline of stateside. Gunners were usually PFCs and Lance Corporals, who loved the action, and were usually anxious to volunteer for flight missions. They would earn extra flight pay while flying with us, and had other regular duties, frequently more mundane, non-combatant roles, which they enjoyed getting a break from the monotony of those jobs.

Unfortunately, there was good reason for the constant feeling of insecurity during the Vietnam conflict. We were never sure of the true allegiance of the Vietnamese people.

As an example, we had been briefed that a new technique being used by the Viet Cong, was to booby trap Zippo cigarette lighters. They would leave them nearby, and if you opened the lid, it would explode. I once was carrying a group of wounded Vietnamese who were supposedly civilians . My crew chief reported the gunner had found a Zippo lighter on the floor of the aircraft, after dropping the wounded at an aid station. We were flying over a river at the time, I told him to toss the lighter out without opening it. When he did, it hit the water and he said it exploded upon water contact. I also had a friend who found a trip wire and booby trap set up under his bed. Fortunately he noticed the wire and called for help to get it disarmed. We also heard of explosive devices placed under the steps of sleeping quarters and grenades tossed into shower areas. Many civilian Vietnamese were authorized to work on base and were supposedly thoroughly vetted, but they were not considered completely trustworthy by most of us.

My tour was pretty typical until the last three months. I was a copilot learning the tactics and operational area for a few months (3-4), then promoted to HAC (Helicopter Aircraft Commander) and toward the end of my tour, Flight Leader (in charge of a flight of two helicopters). As a HAC, I was in charge of the aircraft, its crew and passengers' safety. It was the HAC's responsibility to complete the mission and decide, if the mission was in peril, to get out of harm's way, without sacrificing Marine lives on board and on the ground.

There were times when the mission we were flying should not have been hazardous, but turned threatening. I was flying a routine re-supply mission to a supposed, secure air traffic controlled landing strip. We decided to practice a GCA (Ground Control Approach), an instrument approach guided by an air traffic controller. On a straight and final glide path, no more than a mile from the landing strip, at 500 feet, we flew over an innocent looking farmer working in a rice patty. As we flew overhead, he or she dropped the farming implement, grabbed an AK-47 (Russian or Chinese assault weapon) and began firing at us. Three rounds penetrated the belly of the aircraft. No one aboard was hit, but my crew chief was so upset, he returned fire with his pistol, having little effect other than vent his frustration. We reported the incident to the control tower, for them to take further action.

The CH-46's aircraft body was mainly aluminum sheet metal. Even small caliber arms could easily penetrate the interior of the helicopter, and endanger passengers and crew. Troops being transported knew this, and frequently sat on their helmets to add further protection and hopefully avoid being hit in private areas. Pilots and copilots had armor plated seats, but that wasn't sufficiently reassuring either. Many, including yours truly, placed our holstered side arms between our legs for added protection during flights. An additional insecurity was the unauthorized fire zones established around supposed "friendly villages." When you took fire from them, you could not return fire without getting authorization, and that wasn't granted most of the time. It was considered insanity by everyone exposed to those conditions and part of the frustrations with this supposed war.

    I had an unexpected tense moment at an early point of my tour. It happened while I was flying as a copilot. We were taking four suspected Viet Cong sympathizers to an allied ROK (Republic Of Korea) Marine base. The ROKs were a tough lot, and were rumored to frequently give harsh treatment to captives, especially during interrogation. When we dropped these sympathizers at the landing pad, a Korean officer stood alone awaiting the group of four we were carrying. Since they only had their hands tied behind them, we asked if he had any other soldiers available to guard these prisoners. He said no, but we could leave now. As we prepared to leave, we noticed he had cocked his pistol, and was threatening the prisoners. My pilot questioned his intent. He repeated that we should go now. The pilot called home base to find out what we should do. They directed us to reload the prisoners and bring them back to the base. The ROK officer vigorously objected to our new orders, and called some of his troops for support. The pilot instructed the 50 caliber gunners to "lock and load." The sound of this process (chambering a round), in these powerful guns, got his attention, and he backed off. We loaded the suspected sympathizers back into the aircraft, and got out of there as soon as we could.

A truly hair-raising experience I witnessed was while flying as a new HAC and wingman to my friend, Jack. We frequently flew two helicopters to an especially dangerous extract, where heavy enemy activity was reported in case help or rescue for the lead aircraft was needed. Jack was the copilot in the lead aircraft. They had to do a "SPIE rig" extract, because of heavy canopy (no convenient place to land). They hovered over the site to pick up the recon squad, and were taking heavy fire. As they attempted to pull them out, the strain of trying to get them through those trees and a hydraulic leak caused by enemy fire, was too much. They began to lose turns (rotors slowing) and therefore, losing lift and altitude. They were forced down into the bush and landed, dragging the recon troops through the trees. The Cobras and Huey gunships were swooping in and out, firing rockets and guns to cover them. The pilot radioed our aircraft that they were going to have to dump fuel to lessen their weight for takeoff. The crew chief also had to try and repair or slow the hydraulic leak, while the wounded recon squad, after being dragged through the trees, was getting aboard. The area was going to be saturated with highly flammable jet fuel. They asked the Cobras and Huey gunships to cease cover fire because of all that fuel now surrounding their aircraft.

As designed, I circled overhead at 1,500 feet. I was very concerned for their safety, and assumed we would be coming down to help or rescue them. Miraculously, they completed everything and took off safely. Then everyone on board their aircraft started shooting (both 50-caliber guns, an M60 machine gun in the rear, and the recon squads M16s shooting out the side windows) to suppress the enemy fire. There were tracers going in all directions. We returned to base without any further injuries or aircraft damage. That was an incredibly scary sight to witness and for my buddy Jack to go through. He later told me he could see multiple enemy tracers flying toward the cockpit and assumed they would soon be hit or be in serious trouble. He hoped I was ready to come down to assist them.

There were two incidents, when I especially recall having to make tough decisions as a HAC. One involved a Marine Recon (Special Forces type) Colonel on board for a reconnaissance mission. He wanted me to fly at a lower, less safe altitude. He wished to more clearly see any possible enemy activity. We had been advised not to fly below 1,500 feet over the area being "reconned," because of experienced RPG (rocket propelled grenade) activity. An RPG was one of the most serious threats to helicopters in Vietnam. Although they were not especially accurate weapons, if one did strike the aircraft, the likelihood of critical damage and serious injury was extreme. I advised the Colonel of this, but he insisted on a lower altitude fly-over. He wanted me to fly well below 1,500 feet. When I refused to comply, he became very angry, and told me that it was a "direct order". I told him that I was the HAC, and in charge of the aircraft and crew's safety. Therefore, I was authorized to make this decision over his objections, if I felt it was unnecessarily perilous. He threatened to file charges against me for insubordination, and disobeying a direct order, but I never heard any more about it. We flew the mission at 1500 feet.

Another incident involved my own crisis. I was the HAC, flying resupply missions to high altitude fire bases in late August of 1970. We had mortars aboard and we were delivering them, when an unexpected problem developed. My copilot, Gary, was a recent in country arrival. He needed flight experience, and we took turns flying the aircraft all day. The last approach he flew was going to another high altitude LZ. His approach was too fast, and we were going to overshoot the landing area. I expected him to wave off the approach and make another attempt, when he suddenly pulled back on the stick and added power. That action raised the nose of the aircraft severely, and slowed us down too quickly. At our altitude, the lift capability of the aircraft was significantly diminished. Before I could react, we were losing turns (rotor blades were slowing down) and we began to lose altitude. By the time I took over the controls, we were below the top of the LZ. I tried to regain turns by lowering the collective (power control to engines). This was a technique to regain rotor turns, and eventually increase lift. I had used it successfully in the past on a high altitude LZ. However, before I could get the turns to recover, we struck the hillside.

The ugliest sound I have ever heard was the sound of the rotors striking the ground, and breaking away. We slid down the hillside a bit until the concertina wire, placed there for security, stopped our slide, but we had landed in a mine field and an explosion ruptured our fuel cells. The aircraft caught fire and everyone began to bail out. The crew and copilot exited fairly quickly.

    I looked back to confirm everyone got out and could see the flames in the body of the aircraft. As I first tried to exit, via an emergency door on each side of the cockpit, I could not unlock the emergency release. My crew chief, Charlie, saw my problem and came back to help me get that door open. When it opened I was so excited I forgot to disconnect the radio wires to my helmet. I could not get out with my flight helmet on, so I ditched it into the cockpit and exited the aircraft. As Charlie and I made our way up the hillside, we both got our flight suits caught in the security wire.

    As the mortars we were carrying in the aircraft began to cook off (explode), we quickly made it up that hill, as though the concertina wires did not exist. The crew made it out safely with one minor injury. My copilot broke his arm when he jumped into a fox hole, as the mortars were exploding. Miraculously no one stepped on any mines during the evacuation. Unfortunately, one wounded passenger we were transporting suffered severe burns from the initial fuel explosions, but survived. The aircraft however was a total loss. The intense fire melted it down to scrap metal.

We were lucky, and to this day I owe a debt of gratitude to my crew chief for his selfless assistance in helping to get that door open. He was one of those crew chiefs who had a lot of experience and was a great asset. I believe he was on his second tour and may have opted for a third. I was grateful to find out that he had made it home safely after those multiple tours. I have since made contact with him, and repeated my deepest appreciation to him.

It is standard procedure after a crash for pilots to be tested physically, psychologically and to have a check flight, in order to regain flying status. My tests were uneventful, and I soon returned to the pilot's seat. However, thereafter, my enthusiasm for making a career out of aviation and flying helicopters had diminished.

One benefit of having such a dramatic experience, I was sent on a "crew rest" for three days to Udorn, Thailand. It was a beautiful location with lush green foliage and beautiful accommodations with reliable, friendly people at a Holiday Inn. Unfortunately, I devoured a fresh, green salad (seldom served in country), with lettuce rinsed with local water. I came down with "Montezuma's Revenge" for 24 hours. A condition caused by ingesting water that contains unaccustomed microbes. What a way to spend my first full day of rest time out of country.

An interesting thing happened almost simultaneously with my accident. According to my mother, she heard something crash in my room on a late August day in 1970. She rushed upstairs and saw my picture had fallen off the wall. She was sure something bad had happened to me. She replaced my picture, and put rosary beads around it. We could not nail down the exact date and time, but it was that same period. Eerie!

Everything was not always so serious. There were plenty of times when we were relaxed and well taken care of on base. We had "hooch maids," Vietnamese women who did our laundry and cleaned our sleeping quarters. We had a flag football team for each squadron, and played some pretty competitive games. One story, exemplifying it's a small world, occurred to me during one such game. I was on the sidelines scouting the next team we were to play. A lance corporal came up to me and asked if my name was Don Chretien. I did not recognize him. He told me that his father drove the school bus I used to ride on, back in Biddeford, Maine. It was unbelievable that I'd meet someone from my hometown halfway around the world, in a combat zone.

Waiting for a Mission (45-caliber pistol on hip belt)

We also had many hours of down time due to weather or mission delays. Monsoon season was especially difficult since we often were grounded by heavy storms. During those periods, we'd spend time in the Ready Room playing cards, competing at darts or playing "ace duce" (a popular dice game of that era). Additional waiting time frequently occurred in the field, awaiting troop arrival, or a mission to be launched. We also had SAR (Search & Rescue) missions, standing by in case a downed aircraft and crew needed to be rescued.

I once was sitting on a helo pad at a fire base, awaiting a mission, on a very hot and humid summer day.

We had our flight suit pant legs and sleeves rolled up as far as we could get them. With the front zipper to our flight suits open all the way, we sat outside in the shade of the copter trying to be less uncomfortable. When we were finally cleared to launch, I looked at the outside air temperature gauge, it registered 140 degrees. It was a great relief when we got those rotor blades turning, and got up to altitude where it was much cooler. While flying we were required to wear our flight suits completely covering our skin as well as gloves for fire protection, along with our flight helmets. After a couple of hours flying in and out of LZs, we were usually drenched with sweat in that hot humid climate.

The radio communication with ground troops and home base had to be active at all times when flying. Therefore, scratchy background noise in our helmet speakers was constant. By the end of an especially long day, I usually had a headache from all that radio clutter. After many hours of radio noise, and constant high frequency sounds from the 46's transmission, I eventually developed some permanent high pitch hearing loss.

Vietnam was visually a gorgeous landscape. It had lush green growth everywhere, very high mountains, cascading waterfalls, elephant grass, rice patties, rivers running everywhere, and the South China Sea with waves rolling onto beaches and rock cliff edifices. However, it was also a land pot holed with exploded artillery craters, and potential danger lurking seemingly everywhere. It was difficult to truly appreciate that beauty at that time.

All pilots also had additional duties beyond flying. I was assigned to S-4 (supply & logistics) and was attached to the base photo lab as its representative officer for a while. It was great duty since it was really run well by the gunnery sergeant in charge. There were two young enlisted men who were photographers and developers. They would frequently ride along with us on missions and take photos of the action to be potentially archived and documented as part of the war's history.

All pilots were allowed two weeks of leave out of country during our tour. On one of those weeks, I went to Hong Kong on leave with my buddy, Jack. We spent a week touring the city, enjoying the sights, and purchasing a few things (quality camera equipment, stereos and tape decks, were very cheap there). We also wanted to sample a true family type restaurant, and asked a cabby to take us to one. He scurried in and out of traffic and took a lot of back streets. We were wondering if he was taking us for a joy ride. He finally reached a destination which looked pretty shaky. He confirmed that this was a good place that his family frequented. It was definitely not on the tourist circuit. He told us he'd be back to pick us up in an hour. We took a leap of faith, and got out of the cab. When we walked in, all eyes turned to look at the only Americans in the place. We ordered our meal by pointing to dishes others were having around us. They did not see many Americans at this particular family restaurant. As we awaited our meal, we heard a lot of commotion in the back room, and wondered what was going on. When they brought our food, we asked why all the commotion. They pointed to a knife and fork that they had rummaged around for us. We told them we wanted to eat like they do, and chop sticks were fine with us. It was just a delightful place with great food and wonderful people. As we were finishing our home style Chinese meal, our cabby came in ready to bring us back to our hotel. What a great experience!

All during my tour, rumors circulated that we were going to go home soon. The squadron sent me to the Philippines for Embarkation School (training on how to pack up equipment and personnel to leave a duty station). I loved getting out of country for a week, but feared I might be ultimately responsible for moving us back to the states, a huge undertaking. That was the only time I hoped we not leave "country" early, and we didn't during my tour. HMM-364 was relocated to Santa Ana, CA in March 1971. I left in December, 1970, that was close. U.S involvement continued until 1975 when Saigon fell to the North Vietnamese. A pilot that I had flown with in country (Jerry Berry – now a retired Colonel) had returned to Vietnam in 1975 and transported Saigon embassy personnel and Vietnamese allies with their families in a CH-46 for 17 hours, culminating with the ambassador and his staff.

I finished my 12-month tour in Vietnam having accumulated 560 combat sorties (missions). A sortie was considered the completion of an assigned task and return to base. We frequently flew more than one sortie per day, depending on the complexity and duration of the mission.

CHAPTER 5

The Road Home

At the end of our tours, everyone was given a choice of next preferred location as a result of being in a combat zone. In December of 1970, I returned to the states having chosen Southern California, as my next duty station. I had been writing to Ardis, the young lady I had met before leaving for Vietnam, for the past year, and knew exactly where I wanted to be situated. I was first placed at MCAS El Toro then Santa Ana Air Stations, both in Southern California, as an instructor pilot. This was also very near where Ardis lived and worked.

I owe my Marine Corps experience, and Jack's sister, with giving me the opportunity to meet the love of my life, Ardis Fellmer. On July 31, 1971, we were married in a military wedding ceremony, in Laguna Hills, California.

In addition to flying, my last additional duty in the Corps was as the Squadron Legal Officer, which I thoroughly enjoyed. I advised troops regarding their disciplinary status, and participated in summary and general court marshals. It spurned some thoughts of returning to school, and getting a law degree, or applying for the FBI. My eventual decision, to pursue a corporate business career, was based on wanting to separate myself from the effects of violence, and having the flexibility to return to Maine in the near future. I was ready to get on with the next phase of my life, husband and father.

I left the Marine Corps on December 15, 1972, with

Honorary arch of swords by fellow Marine pilots at St. Nicholas Church

an honorable discharge, as a Captain. I completed my military commitment and had earned a few medals; Air Medal with #28 (indicates number of air medals based on 20 missions per medal), Vietnamese Cross of Gallantry,

Vietnamese Service Medal, Vietnamese Campaign Medal, Meritorious Unit Citation, and National Defense Service Medal. Most of those medals were routine for helo pilots and some had many more than I. I do not consider my contribution as heroic, I just did my duty.

Although Vietnam was not my favorite location, the experience shared with great people, was a highlight of my life in the Corps. During my overseas tour of duty in 1970, I also had the opportunity to see countries, and locations such as: Sydney, Australia, Hong Kong, Thailand, and the Philippines. Australia was by far my favorite country.

That's where I went for my one week R & R. It came halfway through my tour, and therefore, I was more than ready for a break from combat operations. While there, I sent a few stuffed Koala Bears to girls back home, including Ardis. She loved that gesture, and it may have swayed her regarding my true intentions. The Aussies have a great appreciation of U.S. military personnel, and treated us with great respect and gratitude. One particular memory was while walking down a busy street in the King Cross section of Sydney. Jack and I we're asked by a stranger, if we were "Yank" military personnel. He then invited us to join him for free drinks at a nearby bar. Later, we went to a party he knew was going on that evening. It was incredible how good it felt to be so warmly accepted and treated as strong allies.

However, that was not the case upon our return to the states. Before landing in San Francisco, we were advised to change into our civilian clothes, to avoid being harassed by protesters. We did not do that, and proudly stepped onto U.S. soil, in standard military dress. Fortunately, we did not experience any protesting, but many returnees did. We had taken many risks and made many sacrifices, while far away from home for 12 months. The negative attitude toward our returning veterans was not expected or appreciated. For years, it kept me silent regarding my experiences and feelings about serving my country, and especially as a Vietnam veteran.

My most recent honor associated with the Marine Corps was attending the retirement of the aircraft I flew in Vietnam, the CH-46. It had been in service for over 50 years. It was one of the most reliable and durable helicopters in Marine history. It had the reputation of getting troops out of harm's way under less than ideal conditions. Pilots who flew the 46 felt confident of its capability and performance. All crews were invited to attend the formal ceremony, held at the Smithsonian Air & Space Museum in Chantilly, VA, outside of Washington,

D.C. on Aug. 1, 2015. While attending the festivities, Ardis and I got to see a few of my former Vietnam squadron mates. It was a very moving experience, including a fly-in of the last active CH-46, followed by its replacement aircraft, the Osprey (a twin engine fixed wing aircraft that can hover like a helicopter). The Marine Corps band played the Marine Hymn, and a formal passing of the aircraft log books took place before us. There was barely a dry eye among the veteran Marines in attendance. An additional thrill was discovering that specific aircraft, being placed in the Smithsonian, was one that I had actually flown in Vietnam with HMM-364. Log book records were available to find out who had flown that helicopter, and I was on that list. That was and continues to be quite a feeling of pride for me.

As part of this celebration weekend, Ardis and I were invited to an informal gathering at the National Museum of the Marine Corps in Quantico, VA. There were hors d'oeuvres, drinks, and a commemorative tee shirt for us. We got the opportunity to visit with Rick, wife Kay, and Hank, both in my squadron in Vietnam. We have kept in contact over the years and really enjoyed seeing them again. What a great time in an awesome environment. The museum is a must see for any Marine, and should be seen by all Americans. Every conflict Marines have been involved in is displayed with in depth explanations. It depicts the Marine Corps history from inception with great exhibits, including aircraft hanging from the ceiling and a walk through HMM-364, CH-46. It's an inspiration that fills one with pride to be an American, and an appreciation of the sacrifices made for our freedom.

While attending the retirement ceremonies, we stayed at a hotel in Quantico. During morning breakfast, we saw a few lean and superb, physically conditioned young men with "white walls" (heads shaved on both sides). I knew that look, when in basic training I looked like that. When I approached one of the lads, he confirmed my belief. They were OCS candidates at the Marine Base at Quantico, where I had been some 46 years earlier. They were very polite, calling me sir and Ardis ma'am. It was also amazing that one was a hopeful jet pilot on his way to Pensacola after commissioning. We enjoyed talking with them and answering some of their questions, regarding my military history, especially my Vietnam helicopter experience. After meeting these young men, I felt reassured that our country's future was in good hands. We also went over to the base, and toured the area where I attended OCS. We saw the obstacle course where I competed many years ago. Great memories, OOO-RAH !

I have now witnessed how our troops are properly welcomed home from overseas assignments. I have also been thanked for my service by strangers on quite a few occasions. It has happened when wearing my Marine cap, or after they noticed my Marine decals on my car. Some have noticed my license plate which reads XCH46P. We recently celebrated the Marine Corps' 241st birthday on

November 10. I also had a free dinner on Veterans Day at a local restaurant (Applebees). A combination of all these things has finally made me feel vindicated. It confirmed that, at long last, my time in Vietnam and the Marine Corps had been appropriately recognized and appreciated.

Semper Fi !

Epilogue

I asked my 96-year-old mother if she would like to read this story. She took a couple of days to finish it. The next morning, she came to me in tears, gave me a hug, a kiss, and then she handed me this note.

"Don, Son,

I never imagined what you went through. When I watched the news at 11pm each night, I'd see those helicopters flying so low. It was heart breaking! You were very thoughtful and brave to have got your crew off that copter. God must have heard my prayers. You accomplished your wildest dream with a lot of training. I'm proud and grateful that you got back safely. We loved seeing you walk through that door at home.

Love you,
Ma."

Made in the USA
Middletown, DE
08 March 2019